THANK YOU FOR YOUR PURCHASE

EMAIL US AT:

customers@gracefulbydesign.com

TO SHARE YOUR EXPERIENCE, WISHES FOR IMPROVEMENTS, OR SIMPLY HOW YOU ARE ENJOYING THIS PRODUCT OR ANY OF OUR GRACEFUL BY DESIGN PRODUCTS.

FOLLOW US ON INSTAGRAM

@gracefulbydesignllc

FOR NEW PRODUCT RELEASES, AS WELL AS SALES INFORMATION. WANT TO HELP OUR SMALL BUSINESS GROW? TAG US IN A COMMENT OR PICTURE OF HOW YOU ARE USING OUR PRODUCTS.

VISIT **www.gracefulbydesign.com**

FOR MORE INFORMATION OR TO SIGN UP FOR OUR GRACEFUL BY DESIGN NEWSLETTER.

Graceful
BY DESIGN

Copyright © 2023, Graceful by Design. All rights reserved. No part of this publication may be reproduced, stored, distributed, or transmitted in any form or by any means without prior written permission of the publisher, except in the case of brief quotations embodied in critical reviews and certain other non-commercial uses permitted by copyright law. All rights reserved worldwide.

Graceful
BY DESIGN

BIBLE VERSE
MAPPING JOURNAL

A NOTE TO THE BIBLE VERSE MAPPER

Thank you for purchasing Graceful By Design's Bible Verse Mapping Journal. This journal is designed to give you the tools and structure to dive deeper into God's word. Bible verse mapping is dissecting verses through defining keywords and getting a further understanding of the historical context, the origin of the words, cross-references, and other translations. Once you map and gather this information, you have the tools to reflect on what you learned, pray, and find ways to apply this to your life. Whether you are an experienced student of the Bible, new to Bible verse mapping, or new to studying the Bible, this journal will guide you through each step.

Start with deciding a topic you would like to dive into, then decide on the verses you would like to study. Once you have the verses you want to study remember to take time to pray and meditate on the Word for God to speak to your heart. Psalms 119:105 reminds us, "Thy word is a lamp unto my feet, and a light unto my path"

Look to the example provided to understand further how to complete a Bible verse study. If you decide to do an exegesis study on each Bible verse, many online resources support looking up the original Hebrew, Greek, or Aramaic words. For example, you can go to olivetree.com, blueletterbible.org, or studylight.org. Blue Letter and Olive Tree also have phone apps for research. A few commentaries I can recommend are, "The Believer's Bible Commentary by William MacDonald, "Commentary on the Whole Bible" by Matthew Henry, and "Concise Commentary on the Whole Bible" by Arno C. Gaebelein.

Color coding is also a great way to draw connections and organize your research and keywords as you Bible Verse Map. Before you start your first verse, gather your supplies: pen, highlighters, and websites or apps you will be referencing. I have three suggestions for the purchaser of this journal. The first is not to overthink it; start, and you will learn and grow along the way. The second suggestion is to take your time. Some verses might take you longer than a week to study; some might be shorter. Finally, to create consistency in your study, time block or set aside time each day when you can focus and have time to pray, in addition to your study. Enjoy!
Sincerely,

Jenna Coleman

Graceful By Design

BIBLE STUDY TOPICS

ANXIETY & FEAR

Luke 12:22-26
Psalm 27:1
Psalm 55:22
Deuteronomy 31:6
Isaiah 41:13-14
Psalm 46:1
Psalm 118:6-7
Proverbs 29:25
Mark 4:39-40
Psalm 34:7
1 Peter 3:14
Psalm 34:4
Isaiah 41:10
Psalm 56:3
Philippians 4:6-7
John 14:27
2 Timothy 1:7
1 John 4:18
Psalm 94:19
Isaiah 43:1
Proverbs 12:25
Psalm 23:4
Joshua 1:9
Matthew 6:34
Peter 5:6-7
Isaiah 35:4-14.
Deuteronomy 3:22
Revelation 1:17
Mark 5:36
Romans 8:38-39
Zephaniah 3:17
Psalm 91:1-16

FRUITS OF THE SPIRIT

John 15:15
John 15:4-9
Galatians 5:22-23
Matthew 7:15-20
Mark 12:28-30
1 Corinthians 13:4-7
1 Corinthians 13:13
Romans 15:13
Psalm 19:8
Phil 4:6-8
John 14:27
Isaiah 55:8-9
Lamentations 3:22-26
Ephesians 4:2
Colossians 1:9-10
Matthew 25:40
Ephesians 5:8-9
Colossians 3:10
Exodus 34:6
1 Chronicles 16:34
Joshua 24:14-15
Psalms 89:1
Ephesians 3:16-17
Colossians 3:12-14
Matthew 5:5
1 Corinthians 10:31
1 Peter 3:3-4
1 Corinthians 10:13
James 1:19-20
2 Corinthians 10:5

SPIRITUAL GROWTH

2 Peter 3:18
Philippians 1:6
Matthew 5:6
Colossians 1:10
1 Peter 2:2
1 Corinthians 11:1
1 Corinthians 13:11
1 Corinthians 14:20
1 Corinthians 2:6
1 Corinthians 3:8
1 Thessalonians 3:12
1 Timothy 4:7
2 Corinthians 3:18
2 Corinthians 5:17
2 Thessalonians 1:3
2 Timothy 2:15
Acts 17:11
Colossians 3:16
Ephesians 4:13
Ephesians 4:15
Hebrews 5:14
Hebrews 6:1
James 1:2
John 15:5
Luke 2:40
Luke 2:52
Matthew 5:48
Philippians 2:13
Philippians 4:13
Romans 8:29
Corinthians 13: 4-8
1 Corinthians 16:14
1 Peter 4:8
1 John 4: 18-19

BIBLE STUDY TOPICS

DATING

Psalms 119:9
1 Corinthians 7:1-2
2 Corinthians 6: 14-15
Proverbs 4: 23
Romans 12: 1-2
1 Timothy 5:1-2
Proverbs 22:24
2 Timothy 2:22
Proverbs 18: 22
Romans 13:13
Philippians 4:8
Hebrews 13:4
1 Corinthians 6:18
Genesis 2:24
1 Corinthians 13: 4-7

EMPTINESS

Proverbs 4:23
Psalm 51:`0
Psalm 85:6
Psalm 109: 30
Psalm 119: 25
Ezekial 36:26
Hebrew 13:15
Isaiah 25:1

SALVATION

Titus 3:5
Romans 10:9
Acts 4:12
Ephesians 2:8
John 14:6
1 John 1:9
1 John 5:13
1 Peter 2:24
1 Peter 3:21
1 Thessalonians 5:9
2 Corinthians 5:17
2 Corinthians 5:21
2 Corinthians 6:2
2 Peter 3:9
2 Thessalonians 2:13
2 Timothy 1:9
Acts 11:18
Acts 16:31
Acts 2:38
Acts 22:16
Acts 28:28
Ephesians 1:13
Ephesians 2:10
Galatians 2:21
James 2:18
John 1:12
John 3:16
John 3:3
John 3:36
John 3:5
John 5:24
John 6:37
John 6:44
Jonah 2:9

PROMISES FROM GOD

Isaiah 40:31
Psalm 37:3-4
1 Corinthians 10:13
Romans 8:38-39
Joshua 1:9
Matthew 6:33
Romans 8:28
James 4:7-8
2 Corinthians 12:9
Matthew 11:28-29
Deuteronomy 31:6
Isaiah 41:10
Psalm 91:3
Isaiah 52:12
Isaiah 54: 10
Exodus 14:14
James 1:5
Jeremiah 29:11
Matthew 11:28
Romans 6:23
Psalm 9:9
Psalm 16:11
James 1:12

BIBLE STUDY TOPICS

ANGER

Leviticus 19:17-18
James 1:19-20
James 4:1-20
Colossians 3:8
Ephesians 4:26-27
Psalm 37:8
Proverbs 15:18
1 Timothy 2:8
Ecclesiastes 7:9

TEENS

Psalms 119:9
Psalms 119:105
Psalm 25:7
Psalm 46: 5
Proverbs 22:24
1 Corinthians 10:13
1 Corinthians 15:33
Philippians 4:8
1 Timothy 4:12
Deuteronomy 31:6
Ephesians 4:29
Exodus 10:12
Galatians 6:9
Peter 5:5-9
Isaiah 41:10
Jeremiah 29:11
Romans 13:13
Romans 15: 13
Philippians 4:6 & 7
Proverbs 1:8 & 9
Proverbs 3: 5 & 6
Matthew 11:28-30
Ephesians 6:1-3

SADNESS

Psalm 30:5
Psalm 23:4
Psalm 34:18
Psalm 63: 7-8
Psalm 72:26
Psalm 23:4
Jeremiah 29:11
Nehemiah 8:10
John 16: 22
Revelation 21:4

DISCONTENT

1 Thessalonians 5:18
Matthew 6:33
Psalm 37:4
Philippian 4:19
2 Corinthians 12:10
James 4:3
Hebrews 13:5

CREATE YOUR OWN VERSE STUDY

CREATE YOUR OWN VERSE STUDY

 ① John 14:16

KEYWORD MAPPING

EXEGESIS OR OTHER KEYWORDS

said ⑤
④ Past of say: to convey information or to utter words.

way
A road, track, path or street for traveling along.

⑥

② **NKJV**

③ Jesus <u>said</u> to him, "I am the <u>way</u>, the <u>truth</u>, and the <u>life</u>; no one <u>comes</u> to the Father but <u>through</u> me."

comes
To move or travel toward or into a place thought of as near or familiar to the speaker.

through
Means of transportation continuing on to the final destination. To continue toward completion.

⑨ Answered - past of answer: to say or provide a response to something. To deal with or react to something

truth
That which is true or in accordance with fact or reality.

<u>Hebrew</u> - Emmet/Emet - beginning, middle + end

<u>Greek</u> - Alethia(o) - unconcealedness, disclosure

<u>Aramaic</u> - Sharara - means tightly bound together

⑩

life
The phenomenon that distinguishes living organisms from non-living organisms

<u>Greek</u>:
- Bios - Life of physical body
- Psuche - Psychological life of human soul
- Zoe - Uncreated eternal life

Divine Spiritual Life

---

⑦ CONTEXT

WHO WROTE IT John the Apostle
The Lord Jesus' Cousin

WHEN Written 80-90 AD

TO WHOM To all (as a witness)

WHY To show that Jesus of Nazareth was Christ the Son of God & that believers in Him might have eternal life

WHERE Written in Ephesus - takes place in the Roman Empire

⑧ TRANSLATIONS

<u>NIV</u> - Jesus <u>answered</u>, "I am the <u>way</u> and the <u>truth</u> and the <u>life</u>. No one <u>comes</u> to the Father except <u>through</u> me.

<u>KJV</u> - Jesus <u>saith</u> unto him, "I am the <u>way</u>, the <u>truth</u>, and the <u>life</u>: no man <u>cometh</u> unto the Father, but <u>by</u> me.

HOW TO USE THIS JOURNAL

Before beginning any study, I suggest taking a moment to pray asking the Holy Spirit to reveal truth to you and give you a teachable attitude. John 16:13, "But when he, the Spirit of truth, comes, he will guide you into all the truth. He will not speak on his own; he will speak only what he hears, and he will tell you what is yet to come." It is important to remember that beyond the academic study of any topic, the word of God is living. Take this time to quiet yourself before you begin.

1. Write your verse to study here.

2. Write out your verse to begin mapping in the large square here.

3. Highlight or underline keywords.

4. Define the keyword in the smaller squares.

5. Color the smaller square the same color as the highlighted word.

6. Connect the definition to the keyword in the verse.

7. Research to complete the context section.

8. Write 2-3 different translations of the verse & highlight or underline the corresponding keywords.

9. Define the different keywords and connect them to the map in the other keywords section.

10. If you choose to dive deeper you can look up words in Greek, Aramaic or Hebrew to define. Add them in the Exegesis section and connect to the corresponding keyword.

VERSES FOR CROSS REFERENCE &/OR COMMENTARY

John 10:9 - I am the door, if anyone enters through me, he will be saved, and will go in & out & find pasture

Acts 4:12 - And there is salvation in no one else; for there is no other name under heaven that has been given among men by which we must be saved.

Commentary - Jesus is our only access to God & salvation. Our works cannot save us. The scripture is non-negotioable.

WHAT I LEARNED ABOUT GOD?

God is our salvation. He sent His Son and is declaring who He is & why He sent Him. God cares and provides for us all that we need.

WHAT I LEARNED ABOUT MYSELF & MANKIND

We cannot work our way to heaven. Our righteousness cannot lead us to salvation. We have sinned; therefore we are sinners in need of a savior. God sent His Son to make a way for us.

REFLECTION & APPLICATION
WHAT IS GOD TELLING ME & HOW CAN I APPLY IT TO MY LIFE?

When I feel lost, I can remember the Lord sent me the way, the truth & the life. The world can be confusing, but God sent the light of the world to show me the way. Do I trust Him always? When I'm feeling anxious where do I turn? I can have peace & comfort in my salvation through the Lord Jesus Christ.

PRAYER

Dear Heavenly Father,

Thank you for sending your Son. Through your Son I am saved, not by my works, but by yours. I can have peace and comfort in knowing that the Lord Jesus is the way, the truth & the life. Help me to share this truth with others so they may know your Son.

In the name of the Lord Jesus Christ, Amen.

11. Research Cross References of your verse or commentary to help in understanding.

12. What does this verse teach me about God? Does it provide me a view of God?

13. What can I learn about myself or mankind in this verse? Psalm 119: 18 "Open my eyes, that I may see Wondrous things from Your law."

14. Reflection & Application asks you to take a minute to see what God wants to teach you from the passage. 2 Timothy 2:15, "Be diligent to present yourself approved to God, a worker who does not need to be ashamed, rightly dividing the word of truth."

15. Close your study in prayer.

11-13-2023

① Luke 12:22-26

KEYWORD MAPPING

Life ⑤
the period during which a person or thing is alive or exists.

Body
the main part of a person, animal, or plant.

② KJV

22 And he said unto his disciples, Therefore I say unto you, take no thought for your life, what ye shall eat; neither for the body, what ye shall put on. 23 The life is more than meat, and the body is more than raiment. 24 Consider the ravens: for they neither sow nor reap; which neither have storehouse nor barn; and God feedeth them: how much more are ye better than the fowls? 25 And which of you with taking thought can add to his stature one cubit? 26 If ye then be not able to do that thing which is least, why take ye thought for the rest?

Stature
quality or fame gained (as by growth or development)

Reap
to cut (as grain) or clear (as a field) with a sickle, scythe, or machine

EXEGESIS OR OTHER KEYWORDS ⑨

thought
said
unto

Ravens
a large shiny black bird that is larger than the related crow

Sow
to cover with or as if with scattered seed for growing. to plant or scatter for growing.

⑩

⑦ CONTEXT

WHO WROTE IT Luke (Gentile)
WHEN A.D. BC/AD
TO WHOM Everyone
WHY So we know Jesus builds us as man
WHERE Caesarea

⑧ TRANSLATIONS

VERSES FOR CROSS REFERENCE &/OR COMMENTARY

⑪

VIEW OF GOD?

⑫

VIEW OF MANKIND?
VIEW OF SELF?

⑬

REFLECTION & APPLICATION
WHAT IS GOD TELLING ME & HOW CAN I APPLY IT TO MY LIFE?

⑭

PRAYER

⑮

KEYWORD MAPPING

EXEGESIS OR OTHER KEYWORDS

CONTEXT

WHO WROTE IT

WHEN

TO WHOM

WHY

WHERE

TRANSLATIONS

VERSES FOR CROSS REFERENCE &/OR COMMENTARY

VIEW OF GOD?

VIEW OF MANKIND?
VIEW OF SELF?

REFLECTION & APPLICATION
WHAT IS GOD TELLING ME & HOW CAN I APPLY IT TO MY LIFE?

PRAYER

KEYWORD MAPPING

EXEGESIS OR OTHER KEYWORDS

CONTEXT

WHO WROTE IT

WHEN

TO WHOM

WHY

WHERE

TRANSLATIONS

VERSES FOR CROSS REFERENCE &/OR COMMENTARY

VIEW OF GOD?

VIEW OF MANKIND?
VIEW OF SELF?

REFLECTION & APPLICATION
WHAT IS GOD TELLING ME & HOW CAN I APPLY IT TO MY LIFE?

PRAYER

KEYWORD MAPPING

EXEGESIS OR OTHER KEYWORDS

CONTEXT

WHO WROTE IT

WHEN

TO WHOM

WHY

WHERE

TRANSLATIONS

VERSES FOR CROSS REFERENCE &/OR COMMENTARY

_____

VIEW OF GOD?

VIEW OF MANKIND?
VIEW OF SELF?

REFLECTION & APPLICATION
WHAT IS GOD TELLING ME & HOW CAN I APPLY IT TO MY LIFE?

_____

PRAYER

KEYWORD MAPPING

EXEGESIS OR OTHER KEYWORDS

CONTEXT

WHO WROTE IT

WHEN

TO WHOM

WHY

WHERE

TRANSLATIONS

VERSES FOR CROSS REFERENCE &/OR COMMENTARY

VIEW OF GOD?

VIEW OF MANKIND?
VIEW OF SELF?

REFLECTION & APPLICATION
WHAT IS GOD TELLING ME & HOW CAN I APPLY IT TO MY LIFE?

PRAYER

KEYWORD MAPPING

EXEGESIS OR OTHER KEYWORDS

CONTEXT

WHO WROTE IT

WHEN

TO WHOM

WHY

WHERE

TRANSLATIONS

VERSES FOR CROSS REFERENCE &/OR COMMENTARY

VIEW OF GOD?

VIEW OF MANKIND?
VIEW OF SELF?

REFLECTION & APPLICATION
WHAT IS GOD TELLING ME & HOW CAN I APPLY IT TO MY LIFE?

PRAYER

KEYWORD MAPPING

EXEGESIS OR OTHER KEYWORDS

CONTEXT

WHO WROTE IT

WHEN

TO WHOM

WHY

WHERE

TRANSLATIONS

VERSES FOR CROSS REFERENCE &/OR COMMENTARY

VIEW OF GOD?

VIEW OF MANKIND?
VIEW OF SELF?

REFLECTION & APPLICATION
WHAT IS GOD TELLING ME & HOW CAN I APPLY IT TO MY LIFE?

PRAYER

KEYWORD MAPPING

EXEGESIS OR OTHER KEYWORDS

CONTEXT

WHO WROTE IT

WHEN

TO WHOM

WHY

WHERE

TRANSLATIONS

VERSES FOR CROSS REFERENCE &/OR COMMENTARY

VIEW OF GOD?

VIEW OF MANKIND?
VIEW OF SELF?

REFLECTION & APPLICATION
WHAT IS GOD TELLING ME & HOW CAN I APPLY IT TO MY LIFE?

PRAYER

KEYWORD MAPPING

EXEGESIS OR OTHER KEYWORDS

CONTEXT

WHO WROTE IT

WHEN

TO WHOM

WHY

WHERE

TRANSLATIONS

VERSES FOR CROSS REFERENCE &/OR COMMENTARY

VIEW OF GOD?

VIEW OF MANKIND?
VIEW OF SELF?

REFLECTION & APPLICATION
WHAT IS GOD TELLING ME & HOW CAN I APPLY IT TO MY LIFE?

PRAYER

KEYWORD MAPPING

EXEGESIS OR OTHER KEYWORDS

CONTEXT

WHO WROTE IT

WHEN

TO WHOM

WHY

WHERE

TRANSLATIONS

VERSES FOR CROSS REFERENCE &/OR COMMENTARY

VIEW OF GOD?

VIEW OF MANKIND?
VIEW OF SELF?

REFLECTION & APPLICATION
WHAT IS GOD TELLING ME & HOW CAN I APPLY IT TO MY LIFE?

PRAYER

KEYWORD MAPPING

EXEGESIS OR OTHER KEYWORDS

CONTEXT

WHO WROTE IT

WHEN

TO WHOM

WHY

WHERE

TRANSLATIONS

VERSES FOR CROSS REFERENCE &/OR COMMENTARY

VIEW OF GOD?

VIEW OF MANKIND?
VIEW OF SELF?

REFLECTION & APPLICATION
WHAT IS GOD TELLING ME & HOW CAN I APPLY IT TO MY LIFE?

PRAYER

KEYWORD MAPPING

EXEGESIS OR OTHER KEYWORDS

CONTEXT

WHO WROTE IT

WHEN

TO WHOM

WHY

WHERE

TRANSLATIONS

VERSES FOR CROSS REFERENCE &/OR COMMENTARY

VIEW OF GOD?

VIEW OF MANKIND?
VIEW OF SELF?

REFLECTION & APPLICATION
WHAT IS GOD TELLING ME & HOW CAN I APPLY IT TO MY LIFE?

PRAYER

KEYWORD MAPPING

EXEGESIS OR OTHER KEYWORDS

CONTEXT

WHO WROTE IT

WHEN

TO WHOM

WHY

WHERE

TRANSLATIONS

VERSES FOR CROSS REFERENCE &/OR COMMENTARY

VIEW OF GOD?

VIEW OF MANKIND?
VIEW OF SELF?

REFLECTION & APPLICATION
WHAT IS GOD TELLING ME & HOW CAN I APPLY IT TO MY LIFE?

PRAYER

KEYWORD MAPPING

EXEGESIS OR OTHER KEYWORDS

CONTEXT

WHO WROTE IT

WHEN

TO WHOM

WHY

WHERE

TRANSLATIONS

VERSES FOR CROSS REFERENCE &/OR COMMENTARY

VIEW OF GOD?

VIEW OF MANKIND?
VIEW OF SELF?

REFLECTION & APPLICATION
WHAT IS GOD TELLING ME & HOW CAN I APPLY IT TO MY LIFE?

PRAYER

KEYWORD MAPPING

EXEGESIS OR OTHER KEYWORDS

CONTEXT

WHO WROTE IT

WHEN

TO WHOM

WHY

WHERE

TRANSLATIONS

VERSES FOR CROSS REFERENCE &/OR COMMENTARY

VIEW OF GOD?

VIEW OF MANKIND?
VIEW OF SELF?

REFLECTION & APPLICATION
WHAT IS GOD TELLING ME & HOW CAN I APPLY IT TO MY LIFE?

PRAYER

KEYWORD MAPPING

EXEGESIS OR OTHER KEYWORDS

CONTEXT

WHO WROTE IT

WHEN

TO WHOM

WHY

WHERE

TRANSLATIONS

VERSES FOR CROSS REFERENCE &/OR COMMENTARY

VIEW OF GOD?

VIEW OF MANKIND?
VIEW OF SELF?

REFLECTION & APPLICATION
WHAT IS GOD TELLING ME & HOW CAN I APPLY IT TO MY LIFE?

PRAYER

KEYWORD MAPPING

EXEGESIS OR OTHER KEYWORDS

CONTEXT

WHO WROTE IT

WHEN

TO WHOM

WHY

WHERE

TRANSLATIONS

VERSES FOR CROSS REFERENCE &/OR COMMENTARY

VIEW OF GOD?

VIEW OF MANKIND?
VIEW OF SELF?

REFLECTION & APPLICATION
WHAT IS GOD TELLING ME & HOW CAN I APPLY IT TO MY LIFE?

PRAYER

KEYWORD MAPPING

EXEGESIS OR OTHER KEYWORDS

CONTEXT

WHO WROTE IT

WHEN

TO WHOM

WHY

WHERE

TRANSLATIONS

VERSES FOR CROSS REFERENCE &/OR COMMENTARY

_____
_____
_____
_____
_____
_____

VIEW OF GOD?

VIEW OF MANKIND?
VIEW OF SELF?

REFLECTION & APPLICATION
WHAT IS GOD TELLING ME & HOW CAN I APPLY IT TO MY LIFE?

_____
_____
_____

PRAYER

_____
_____
_____
_____

KEYWORD MAPPING

EXEGESIS OR OTHER KEYWORDS

CONTEXT

WHO WROTE IT

WHEN

TO WHOM

WHY

WHERE

TRANSLATIONS

VERSES FOR CROSS REFERENCE &/OR COMMENTARY

VIEW OF GOD?

VIEW OF MANKIND?
VIEW OF SELF?

REFLECTION & APPLICATION
WHAT IS GOD TELLING ME & HOW CAN I APPLY IT TO MY LIFE?

PRAYER

KEYWORD MAPPING

EXEGESIS OR OTHER KEYWORDS

CONTEXT

WHO WROTE IT

WHEN

TO WHOM

WHY

WHERE

TRANSLATIONS

VERSES FOR CROSS REFERENCE &/OR COMMENTARY

VIEW OF GOD?

VIEW OF MANKIND?
VIEW OF SELF?

REFLECTION & APPLICATION
WHAT IS GOD TELLING ME & HOW CAN I APPLY IT TO MY LIFE?

PRAYER

KEYWORD MAPPING

EXEGESIS OR OTHER KEYWORDS

CONTEXT

WHO WROTE IT

WHEN

TO WHOM

WHY

WHERE

TRANSLATIONS

VERSES FOR CROSS REFERENCE &/OR COMMENTARY

VIEW OF GOD?

VIEW OF MANKIND?
VIEW OF SELF?

REFLECTION & APPLICATION
WHAT IS GOD TELLING ME & HOW CAN I APPLY IT TO MY LIFE?

PRAYER

KEYWORD MAPPING

EXEGESIS OR OTHER KEYWORDS

CONTEXT

WHO WROTE IT

WHEN

TO WHOM

WHY

WHERE

TRANSLATIONS

VERSES FOR CROSS REFERENCE &/OR COMMENTARY

VIEW OF GOD?

VIEW OF MANKIND?
VIEW OF SELF?

REFLECTION & APPLICATION
WHAT IS GOD TELLING ME & HOW CAN I APPLY IT TO MY LIFE?

PRAYER

KEYWORD MAPPING

EXEGESIS OR OTHER KEYWORDS

CONTEXT

WHO WROTE IT

WHEN

TO WHOM

WHY

WHERE

TRANSLATIONS

VERSES FOR CROSS REFERENCE &/OR COMMENTARY

VIEW OF GOD?

VIEW OF MANKIND?
VIEW OF SELF?

REFLECTION & APPLICATION
WHAT IS GOD TELLING ME & HOW CAN I APPLY IT TO MY LIFE?

PRAYER

KEYWORD MAPPING

EXEGESIS OR OTHER KEYWORDS

CONTEXT

WHO WROTE IT

WHEN

TO WHOM

WHY

WHERE

TRANSLATIONS

VERSES FOR CROSS REFERENCE &/OR COMMENTARY

VIEW OF GOD?

VIEW OF MANKIND?
VIEW OF SELF?

REFLECTION & APPLICATION
WHAT IS GOD TELLING ME & HOW CAN I APPLY IT TO MY LIFE?

PRAYER

KEYWORD MAPPING

EXEGESIS OR OTHER KEYWORDS

CONTEXT

WHO WROTE IT

WHEN

TO WHOM

WHY

WHERE

TRANSLATIONS

VERSES FOR CROSS REFERENCE &/OR COMMENTARY

VIEW OF GOD?

VIEW OF MANKIND?
VIEW OF SELF?

REFLECTION & APPLICATION
WHAT IS GOD TELLING ME & HOW CAN I APPLY IT TO MY LIFE?

PRAYER

KEYWORD MAPPING

EXEGESIS OR OTHER KEYWORDS

CONTEXT

WHO WROTE IT

WHEN

TO WHOM

WHY

WHERE

TRANSLATIONS

VERSES FOR CROSS REFERENCE &/OR COMMENTARY

VIEW OF GOD?

VIEW OF MANKIND?
VIEW OF SELF?

REFLECTION & APPLICATION
WHAT IS GOD TELLING ME & HOW CAN I APPLY IT TO MY LIFE?

PRAYER

KEYWORD MAPPING

EXEGESIS OR OTHER KEYWORDS

CONTEXT

WHO WROTE IT

WHEN

TO WHOM

WHY

WHERE

TRANSLATIONS

VERSES FOR CROSS REFERENCE &/OR COMMENTARY

VIEW OF GOD?

VIEW OF MANKIND?
VIEW OF SELF?

REFLECTION & APPLICATION
WHAT IS GOD TELLING ME & HOW CAN I APPLY IT TO MY LIFE?

PRAYER

KEYWORD MAPPING

EXEGESIS OR OTHER KEYWORDS

CONTEXT

WHO WROTE IT

WHEN

TO WHOM

WHY

WHERE

TRANSLATIONS

VERSES FOR CROSS REFERENCE &/OR COMMENTARY

VIEW OF GOD?

VIEW OF MANKIND?
VIEW OF SELF?

REFLECTION & APPLICATION
WHAT IS GOD TELLING ME & HOW CAN I APPLY IT TO MY LIFE?

PRAYER

KEYWORD MAPPING

EXEGESIS OR OTHER KEYWORDS

CONTEXT

WHO WROTE IT

WHEN

TO WHOM

WHY

WHERE

TRANSLATIONS

VERSES FOR CROSS REFERENCE &/OR COMMENTARY

VIEW OF GOD?

VIEW OF MANKIND?
VIEW OF SELF?

REFLECTION & APPLICATION
WHAT IS GOD TELLING ME & HOW CAN I APPLY IT TO MY LIFE?

PRAYER

KEYWORD MAPPING

EXEGESIS OR OTHER KEYWORDS

CONTEXT

WHO WROTE IT

WHEN

TO WHOM

WHY

WHERE

TRANSLATIONS

VERSES FOR CROSS REFERENCE &/OR COMMENTARY

_____
_____
_____
_____
_____
_____
_____

VIEW OF GOD?   ### VIEW OF MANKIND?
                                    VIEW OF SELF?

REFLECTION & APPLICATION
WHAT IS GOD TELLING ME & HOW CAN I APPLY IT TO MY LIFE?

_____
_____
_____
_____

PRAYER

_____
_____
_____
_____
_____

KEYWORD MAPPING

EXEGESIS OR OTHER KEYWORDS

CONTEXT

WHO WROTE IT

WHEN

TO WHOM

WHY

WHERE

TRANSLATIONS

VERSES FOR CROSS REFERENCE &/OR COMMENTARY

VIEW OF GOD?

VIEW OF MANKIND?
VIEW OF SELF?

REFLECTION & APPLICATION
WHAT IS GOD TELLING ME & HOW CAN I APPLY IT TO MY LIFE?

PRAYER

KEYWORD MAPPING

EXEGESIS OR OTHER KEYWORDS

CONTEXT

WHO WROTE IT

WHEN

TO WHOM

WHY

WHERE

TRANSLATIONS

VERSES FOR CROSS REFERENCE &/OR COMMENTARY

VIEW OF GOD?

VIEW OF MANKIND?
VIEW OF SELF?

REFLECTION & APPLICATION
WHAT IS GOD TELLING ME & HOW CAN I APPLY IT TO MY LIFE?

PRAYER

KEYWORD MAPPING

EXEGESIS OR OTHER KEYWORDS

CONTEXT

WHO WROTE IT

WHEN

TO WHOM

WHY

WHERE

TRANSLATIONS

VERSES FOR CROSS REFERENCE &/OR COMMENTARY

VIEW OF GOD?

VIEW OF MANKIND?
VIEW OF SELF?

REFLECTION & APPLICATION
WHAT IS GOD TELLING ME & HOW CAN I APPLY IT TO MY LIFE?

PRAYER

KEYWORD MAPPING

EXEGESIS OR OTHER KEYWORDS

CONTEXT

WHO WROTE IT

WHEN

TO WHOM

WHY

WHERE

TRANSLATIONS

VERSES FOR CROSS REFERENCE &/OR COMMENTARY

VIEW OF GOD?

VIEW OF MANKIND?
VIEW OF SELF?

REFLECTION & APPLICATION
WHAT IS GOD TELLING ME & HOW CAN I APPLY IT TO MY LIFE?

PRAYER

KEYWORD MAPPING

EXEGESIS OR OTHER KEYWORDS

CONTEXT

WHO WROTE IT

WHEN

TO WHOM

WHY

WHERE

TRANSLATIONS

VERSES FOR CROSS REFERENCE &/OR COMMENTARY

VIEW OF GOD?

VIEW OF MANKIND?
VIEW OF SELF?

REFLECTION & APPLICATION
WHAT IS GOD TELLING ME & HOW CAN I APPLY IT TO MY LIFE?

PRAYER

KEYWORD MAPPING

EXEGESIS OR OTHER KEYWORDS

CONTEXT

WHO WROTE IT

WHEN

TO WHOM

WHY

WHERE

TRANSLATIONS

VERSES FOR CROSS REFERENCE &/OR COMMENTARY

VIEW OF GOD?

VIEW OF MANKIND?
VIEW OF SELF?

REFLECTION & APPLICATION
WHAT IS GOD TELLING ME & HOW CAN I APPLY IT TO MY LIFE?

PRAYER

KEYWORD MAPPING

EXEGESIS OR OTHER KEYWORDS

CONTEXT

WHO WROTE IT

WHEN

TO WHOM

WHY

WHERE

TRANSLATIONS

VERSES FOR CROSS REFERENCE &/OR COMMENTARY

VIEW OF GOD?

VIEW OF MANKIND?
VIEW OF SELF?

REFLECTION & APPLICATION
WHAT IS GOD TELLING ME & HOW CAN I APPLY IT TO MY LIFE?

PRAYER

KEYWORD MAPPING

EXEGESIS OR OTHER KEYWORDS

CONTEXT

WHO WROTE IT

WHEN

TO WHOM

WHY

WHERE

TRANSLATIONS

VERSES FOR CROSS REFERENCE &/OR COMMENTARY

VIEW OF GOD?

VIEW OF MANKIND?
VIEW OF SELF?

REFLECTION & APPLICATION
WHAT IS GOD TELLING ME & HOW CAN I APPLY IT TO MY LIFE?

PRAYER

KEYWORD MAPPING

EXEGESIS OR OTHER KEYWORDS

CONTEXT

WHO WROTE IT

WHEN

TO WHOM

WHY

WHERE

TRANSLATIONS

VERSES FOR CROSS REFERENCE &/OR COMMENTARY

VIEW OF GOD?

VIEW OF MANKIND?
VIEW OF SELF?

REFLECTION & APPLICATION
WHAT IS GOD TELLING ME & HOW CAN I APPLY IT TO MY LIFE?

PRAYER

KEYWORD MAPPING

EXEGESIS OR OTHER KEYWORDS

CONTEXT

WHO WROTE IT

WHEN

TO WHOM

WHY

WHERE

TRANSLATIONS

VERSES FOR CROSS REFERENCE &/OR COMMENTARY

VIEW OF GOD?

VIEW OF MANKIND?
VIEW OF SELF?

REFLECTION & APPLICATION
WHAT IS GOD TELLING ME & HOW CAN I APPLY IT TO MY LIFE?

PRAYER

KEYWORD MAPPING

EXEGESIS OR OTHER KEYWORDS

CONTEXT

WHO WROTE IT

WHEN

TO WHOM

WHY

WHERE

TRANSLATIONS

VERSES FOR CROSS REFERENCE &/OR COMMENTARY

VIEW OF GOD?

VIEW OF MANKIND?
VIEW OF SELF?

REFLECTION & APPLICATION
WHAT IS GOD TELLING ME & HOW CAN I APPLY IT TO MY LIFE?

PRAYER

KEYWORD MAPPING

EXEGESIS OR OTHER KEYWORDS

CONTEXT

WHO WROTE IT

WHEN

TO WHOM

WHY

WHERE

TRANSLATIONS

VERSES FOR CROSS REFERENCE &/OR COMMENTARY

VIEW OF GOD?

VIEW OF MANKIND?
VIEW OF SELF?

REFLECTION & APPLICATION
WHAT IS GOD TELLING ME & HOW CAN I APPLY IT TO MY LIFE?

PRAYER

KEYWORD MAPPING

EXEGESIS OR OTHER KEYWORDS

CONTEXT

WHO WROTE IT

WHEN

TO WHOM

WHY

WHERE

TRANSLATIONS

VERSES FOR CROSS REFERENCE &/OR COMMENTARY

VIEW OF GOD?

VIEW OF MANKIND?
VIEW OF SELF?

REFLECTION & APPLICATION
WHAT IS GOD TELLING ME & HOW CAN I APPLY IT TO MY LIFE?

PRAYER

KEYWORD MAPPING

EXEGESIS OR OTHER KEYWORDS

CONTEXT

WHO WROTE IT

WHEN

TO WHOM

WHY

WHERE

TRANSLATIONS

VERSES FOR CROSS REFERENCE &/OR COMMENTARY

VIEW OF GOD?

VIEW OF MANKIND?
VIEW OF SELF?

REFLECTION & APPLICATION
WHAT IS GOD TELLING ME & HOW CAN I APPLY IT TO MY LIFE?

PRAYER

KEYWORD MAPPING

EXEGESIS OR OTHER KEYWORDS

CONTEXT

WHO WROTE IT

WHEN

TO WHOM

WHY

WHERE

TRANSLATIONS

VERSES FOR CROSS REFERENCE &/OR COMMENTARY

VIEW OF GOD?

VIEW OF MANKIND?
VIEW OF SELF?

REFLECTION & APPLICATION
WHAT IS GOD TELLING ME & HOW CAN I APPLY IT TO MY LIFE?

PRAYER

KEYWORD MAPPING

EXEGESIS OR OTHER KEYWORDS

CONTEXT

WHO WROTE IT

WHEN

TO WHOM

WHY

WHERE

TRANSLATIONS

VERSES FOR CROSS REFERENCE &/OR COMMENTARY

VIEW OF GOD?

VIEW OF MANKIND?
VIEW OF SELF?

REFLECTION & APPLICATION
WHAT IS GOD TELLING ME & HOW CAN I APPLY IT TO MY LIFE?

PRAYER

KEYWORD MAPPING

EXEGESIS OR OTHER KEYWORDS

CONTEXT

WHO WROTE IT

WHEN

TO WHOM

WHY

WHERE

TRANSLATIONS

VERSES FOR CROSS REFERENCE &/OR COMMENTARY

VIEW OF GOD?

VIEW OF MANKIND?
VIEW OF SELF?

REFLECTION & APPLICATION
WHAT IS GOD TELLING ME & HOW CAN I APPLY IT TO MY LIFE?

PRAYER

KEYWORD MAPPING

EXEGESIS OR OTHER KEYWORDS

CONTEXT

WHO WROTE IT

WHEN

TO WHOM

WHY

WHERE

TRANSLATIONS

VERSES FOR CROSS REFERENCE &/OR COMMENTARY

VIEW OF GOD?

VIEW OF MANKIND?
VIEW OF SELF?

REFLECTION & APPLICATION
WHAT IS GOD TELLING ME & HOW CAN I APPLY IT TO MY LIFE?

PRAYER

KEYWORD MAPPING

EXEGESIS OR OTHER KEYWORDS

CONTEXT

WHO WROTE IT

WHEN

TO WHOM

WHY

WHERE

TRANSLATIONS

VERSES FOR CROSS REFERENCE &/OR COMMENTARY

VIEW OF GOD?

VIEW OF MANKIND?
VIEW OF SELF?

REFLECTION & APPLICATION
WHAT IS GOD TELLING ME & HOW CAN I APPLY IT TO MY LIFE?

PRAYER

KEYWORD MAPPING

EXEGESIS OR
OTHER KEYWORDS

CONTEXT

WHO WROTE IT

WHEN

TO WHOM

WHY

WHERE

TRANSLATIONS

VERSES FOR CROSS REFERENCE &/OR COMMENTARY

VIEW OF GOD?

VIEW OF MANKIND?
VIEW OF SELF?

REFLECTION & APPLICATION
WHAT IS GOD TELLING ME & HOW CAN I APPLY IT TO MY LIFE?

PRAYER

KEYWORD MAPPING

EXEGESIS OR OTHER KEYWORDS

CONTEXT

WHO WROTE IT

WHEN

TO WHOM

WHY

WHERE

TRANSLATIONS

VERSES FOR CROSS REFERENCE &/OR COMMENTARY

VIEW OF GOD?

VIEW OF MANKIND?
VIEW OF SELF?

REFLECTION & APPLICATION
WHAT IS GOD TELLING ME & HOW CAN I APPLY IT TO MY LIFE?

PRAYER

KEYWORD MAPPING

EXEGESIS OR OTHER KEYWORDS

CONTEXT

WHO WROTE IT

WHEN

TO WHOM

WHY

WHERE

TRANSLATIONS

VERSES FOR CROSS REFERENCE &/OR COMMENTARY

VIEW OF GOD?

VIEW OF MANKIND?
VIEW OF SELF?

REFLECTION & APPLICATION
WHAT IS GOD TELLING ME & HOW CAN I APPLY IT TO MY LIFE?

PRAYER

PRAYER LIST & PRAISES
WHAT AM I PRAYING FOR AND WHAT AM I THANKFUL FOR

PRAYER LIST & PRAISES
WHAT AM I PRAYING FOR AND WHAT AM I THANKFUL FOR

PRAYER LIST & PRAISES
WHAT AM I PRAYING FOR AND WHAT AM I THANKFUL FOR

PRAYER LIST & PRAISES
WHAT AM I PRAYING FOR AND WHAT AM I THANKFUL FOR

PRAYER LIST & PRAISES
WHAT AM I PRAYING FOR AND WHAT AM I THANKFUL FOR

PRAYER LIST & PRAISES
WHAT AM I PRAYING FOR AND WHAT AM I THANKFUL FOR

PRAYER LIST & PRAISES
WHAT AM I PRAYING FOR AND WHAT AM I THANKFUL FOR

PRAYER LIST & PRAISES
WHAT AM I PRAYING FOR AND WHAT AM I THANKFUL FOR

PRAYER LIST & PRAISES
WHAT AM I PRAYING FOR AND WHAT AM I THANKFUL FOR

PRAYER LIST & PRAISES
WHAT AM I PRAYING FOR AND WHAT AM I THANKFUL FOR

Copyright © 2023, Graceful by Design. All rights reserved. No part of this publication may be reproduced, stored, distributed, or transmitted in any form or by any means without prior written permission of the publisher, except in the case of brief quotations embodied in critical reviews and certain other non-commercial uses permitted by copyright law. All rights reserved worldwide.

Made in the USA
Middletown, DE
26 June 2023

33455627R00071